I0440093

# Unleashing Technology Innovations for Positive Human-animal Relationships:

## Tales from AnimalHack 2023

Sarasa Ouchi, Yuma Karube, and Banri Ouchi
(Editors)

Binnovative Innovation Book Series

AnimalHack Logo Design:   Sougou Tojima
Cover Design:             Banri Ouchi

Copyright © 2023 Binnovative

https://www.binnovative.org/

All rights reserved.

ISBN: 979-8-8722-5466-9

# Table of Contents

# Foreword

As Binnovative's CEO, I am grateful for the opportunity to contribute to AnimalHack, an event organized and run by passionate students around the US. It was a rewarding experience to serve as one of the judges for this hackathon, and I was impressed by the multitude of enthusiastic attendees who presented innovative ideas around a topic close to their hearts.

What amazed me was the young organizing team's decision to center the hackathon theme around animals. Their choice reflects a commitment to fostering innovation driven by a genuine love for animals.

At Binnovative, our mission is to "Collaborate to Innovate – cultivating the entrepreneurial mindset by fostering international, intercultural, and collaborative experiences in innovation ecosystems." In alignment with this mission, we organize various collaborative events, and it brought me immense joy to support an event initiated by the original attendees of a previous event we organized. I am proud of their dedicated efforts in organizing AnimalHack.

I eagerly anticipate the next edition of AnimalHack in the coming year! I hope that more individuals will join in developing solutions for this important cause that resonates with many of us. I firmly believe that through collective effort, we can make a positive impact and contribute to changing the world for the better.

Eriko Nishimoto
Founder and CEO of Binnovative

# Preface

This book collects some of the award-winning projects from Animal-Hack 2023. AnimalHack is a student-organized online hackathon for anyone who interacts with any animals - including pets, service animals, farm animals and wild animals. We were disappointed with the lack of international, open hackathons that focus on animals, so we started our own.

The inaugural edition of AnimalHack took place on September 10, 2023. For its launch, we formed a team of the following six organizers from the Boston and Seattle areas this June.

- Yuma Karube (co-chair)
- Yua Murakami
- Banri Ouchi
- Sarasa Ouchi (co-chair)
- Hanna Suzuki
- Sougou Tojima

We started by organizing an online meeting to decide a name for the hackathon. Each of us brought ideas for a name that would best fit the themes of the hackathon, and we came up with the name we have now after much deliberation. Then, we divided up the roles and designed a logo for the hackathon, produced hackathon swags with the logo, built the hackathon Web site at `https://AnimalHack.org/`, set up a DevPost.com page for announcements, created a Discord community to communicate with participants, prepared an online registration page for project presentations, formed a panel of judges, and created certificates for those who participated. We spent three months preparing for the event.

AnimalHack 2023 attracted 263 participants at DevPost.com. We received 29 project submissions, and 11 of them presented their projects at the hackathon event. They gathered online from four countries in North America, Asia and Africa and gave 10-minute presentations each in front of judges and other hackathon participants. At the end of the event, judges announced the following prize winners. Congratulations!

- Grand Prix (1st place):
  - Yuma Karube, "Hydrate Cat"
- Silver Prize (2nd place):
  - Shun and Rei Nagata, "Squirrel Repeller"
- Bronze Prize (3rd place):
  - Soham Vij, "Pet Picker - A Simple Approach to Finding Your Perfect Pet"
- Honorable Mentions:
  - Hanna Suzuki, "Cloud-assisted Electronic Deer Repeller"
  - Tyo An, "Pawprint"
  - Shuntaro Sato, "Motorized scarecrow with infrared laser detection system and camera"
  - Udogwu Emiri and Grace Okunomo, "Celo Pets"
- Excellence in Creativity Award:
  - Zana Yan, "Petupia"
- Emerging Talent Award:
  - Dharshini Venkatesan, "Virtual Pet Adoption Center"

We contacted these prize winners to see if they are interested in publishing book chapters that summarize their projects. Upon their responses, we planned 5 chapters and received 4 of them. This book includes those 4 chapters.

Chapter 1, entitled "Cloud-assisted Electronic Deer Repeller," is authored by Hanna Suzuki. It addresses a nuisance issue where wild deer damage home gardens and describes an outdoor, in-garden system that distributes liquid repellent around garden plants with a Raspberry Pi computer, liquid pumps, Python and a cloud data storage.

In Chapter 2, Shun and Rei Nagata also address nuisance by wild animals, especially squirrels. Their Raspberry Pi-powered system, the Squirrel Repeller, operates a motion sensor to detect wild animals that try to damage garden plants, takes pictures of them, and runs a servo motor to spin a wooden stick to scare them away.

Chapter 3 reports the Hydrate Cat project, which Yuma Karube worked on to address the wellbeing of domestic cats, particularly in a hydration point of view. Using a Raspberry Pi and its peripherals such as a weight sensor, his system monitors a cat's daily water intake, records it in a cloud data storage, and visualizes time-series water intakes as graphs. It is intended to provide cat owners with data-driven insights on whether their cats stay well-hydrated.

In Chapter 4, Soham Vij describes his multi-criteria search service for pet adoption. To match pets with the right owners, it runs searches and makes suggestions based on given preferences on maintenance, sociability, life expectancy, diet compatibility and price. Its informative and mobile-friendly data display is implemented with HTML 5, Cascading Style Sheets (CSS) and JavaScript.

Our special thanks go to our judges, Namaswi Chandarana and Eriko Nishimoto, for their active interaction with hackathon participants and their professional judgment on prize winners.

We also appreciate Binnovative and the AnimalHack Advisory Board for helping us organize AnimalHack 2023 successfully and complete our hackathon journey with this book publication. We hope you will find this book informative, enjoyable, and inspiring!

Sarasa Ouchi, Yuma Karube, and Banri Ouchi

December 2023

# Call for Contributions to AnimalHack

https://AnimalHack.org/

AnimalHack is a student-organized hackathon for anyone who inter-acts with any animals - including pets, service animals, farm animals and wild animals. We were disappointed with the lack of international, open hackathons that focus on animals, so we started our own in 2023.

AnimalHack is a platform that inspires you to think of needs, wants and challenges in interacting with animals. It is intended to help you ignite creative solutions (hacks) with technology and innovate human-animal relationships.

AnimalHack welcomes anyone of all ages and all technical skills, from limited experience to advanced. Entry is free.

Expected project topics include, but are not limited to:

- Contributing to animal wellbeing
- Assisting animal owners
- Assisting animal adoptions
- Monitoring, conserving and improving the environment around animals
- Observing, tracing, and protecting wild animals
- Breeding, rearing/farming and harvesting animals
- Managing nuisance issues with wildlife
- Addressing animal abuse, cruelty, and illegal capture/trade

Solutions can take many different forms such as apps, games, social platforms, web sites/services, devices, robots, data collection/storage, data analysis/forecasts, data visualization, information retrieval, and 3-dimensional modeling/printing.

AnimalHack takes place annually – usually in early fall. It is hosted by Binnovative, a nonprofit organization in Massachusetts, USA.

# Cloud-assisted Electronic Deer Repeller

Hanna Suzuki

John Glenn Middle School
Bedford, MA 01730, USA

## Abstract

This project builds an electronic deer repeller, called The Ultimate Deer Repeller (TUDR), to address a nuisance issue where wild deer damage home gardens. TUDR is an outdoor, in-garden system that distributes liquid repellent around garden plants with liquid pumps controlled by a Raspberry Pi computer. It runs a Python program that periodically contacts a cloud database and triggers repellent distribution. The database's data entry form allows gardeners to remotely set up and adjust the repellent distribution schedule with their smartphones, tablets, or web browsers.

## 1.1 Introduction

Gardening is a popular family activity all over the world. It is a rewarding way to enjoy the sights and smells of nature. It is refreshing, calming, and produces something beautiful and healthy.

However, growing flowers, vegetables, fruits and other plants in yards comes with its own consequences such as nuisance issues by wildlife. Although they are an important part of the ecosystem, many wildlife species can become a nuisance when in close proximity to humans.

Some wild animals can damage flowerbeds, vegetable gardens and fruit patches in residential properties: nibbling flowers and leaves,

1

destroying crops and digging up flower bulbs. In the United States, those responsible wildlife includes deer, groundhogs, racoons, rabbits, and squirrels. Of these species, deer are perhaps the most destructive nuisance.

Deer are large animals that eat well over 700 species of plants [1]. They usually feed in the late evening and early morning; it is not easy to observe them. However, in suburban areas where deer have become accustomed to people, they may be active throughout the day.

In the US, white-tailed deer are the most abundant and best-known deer species [2]. They are named after the white underside of their tail, which they raise and flare when alarmed to warn other deer. They are powerful enough to damage a garden significantly in a short amount of time [3].

In Massachusetts, it is estimated that there are more than 150,000 deer herded across the state [2]. In most of central and western Massachusetts, there are 12 to 18 deer per square mile, which is a reasonable and acceptable density [4]. There are more than 30 to 50 deer per square mile in areas of eastern Massachusetts where hunting is restricted [4]. Additionally, deer are increasing both their population and habitat range [3, 5]. In some parts of the state, particularly southeastern Massachusetts, the population increases by 15% per year [1].

According to the US National Wildlife Federation, deer can damage a garden in several ways [6]:

- They may nibble flowers, leaves and fresh/tender small stems of plants. They leave ragged edges on remaining plant parts. While they are often attracted to highly palatable plants like roses, tulips, lilies, impatiens and sunflowers, they also like broad-leaved flowering plants such as hostas. In a state-wide survey in Connecticut, 97% of gardeners noted their hostas had been browsed by deer [5].

- They may consume the terminal and lateral buds of shrubs and trees. Yew, euonymus and arborvitae were the most susceptible species in a state-wide survey in Connecticut [5].

- They may eat entire plants such as leafy vegetables (e.g., lettuce and cabbage), fruits (e.g., apples) and legumes.

- They may trample plants and damage them beyond repair. Adult male deer weigh an average of 120 to 160 pounds, while females average 80 to 120 pounds [2].

These damages can quickly transform gardens from points of joy and pride to scenes of devastation. For example, when deer browse hostas, they eat the flowers and leaves only, leaving the stems. This results in aesthetic devastation because the hostas look like a bunch of celery sticking out of the ground (Fig. 1).

Fig. 1: Damaged Hostas [7]

More importantly, the damaged hostas may not be able to survive the winter, even though they are perennials. This would cost time and money for replanting in spring. The estimated annual economic loss to residential and commercial ornamental plants was 49 million dollars for the state of New York [8].

## 1.2 Background

Fencing is considered the most effective long-term strategy to minimize deer browse damage [9]. However, installing a fence around a garden may be too time-consuming and expensive for gardeners. Also, its appearance may not be acceptable for ornamental plants.

In terms of cost and appearance, motion-activated lights and motion-activated ultrasonic devices have advantages. However, deer are often smart enough to become tolerant of them. (Deer can become tolerant of even humans).

Another strategy is to use repellents - compounds based on natural or artificial materials to repel deer. Of various types of repellents, odor-based ones are reportedly the most effective [10].

Despite their effectiveness, odor-based repellents have three issues in practice. First, their effectiveness is temporary. It degrades gradually over time, after being applied, and drops significantly by rainfall. Repellents have to be reapplied regularly. Another issue is that they have to be consistently applied on/around all the plants to be protected. If applied after deer damage has occurred, they likely will not repel deer from something they have already eaten [1]. The third issue is that their odor is terrible for humans as well. In case their clothes become smelly, gardeners often put on extra disposable layers to spray repellents onto/around plants (Fig. 2).

Fig. 2: Odor-based Repellent being Sprayed onto Hostas

## 1.3 The Ultimate Deer Repeller (TUDR)

This project builds an electronic deer repeller, called The Ultimate Deer Repeller (TUDR), to keep deer out of residential properties by solving the three issues described in Section 1.2. TUDR is an outdoor, in-garden system that automatically distributes liquid repellent around plants with liquid pumps and tubes (Fig. 3).

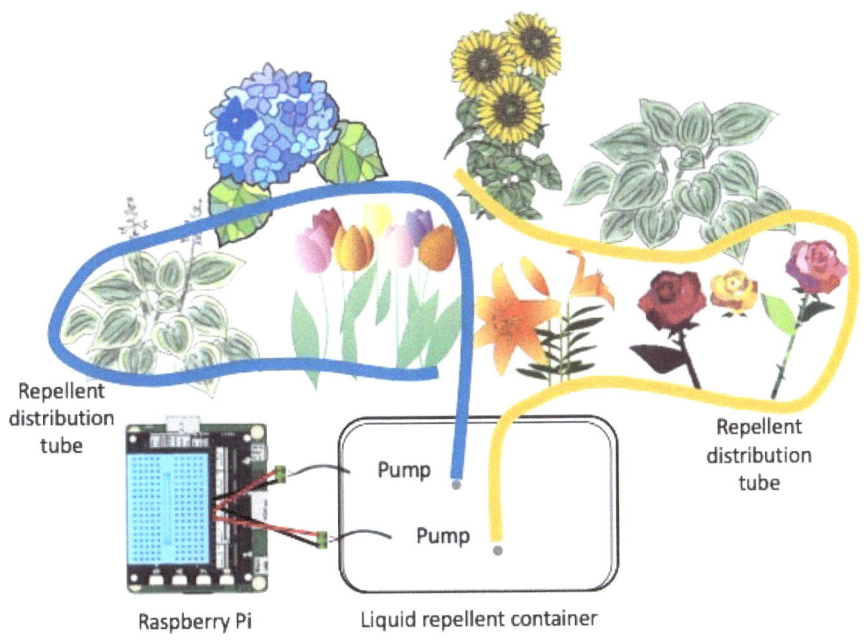

Fig. 3: TUDR System Overview

A key component in TUDR is a small (credit card sized) computer called Raspberry Pi. It runs a Python program that periodically contacts a cloud database called Kintone (**https://kintone.dev**) and controls liquid pumps to trigger repellent distribution. The database's data entry form allows gardeners to remotely set up and adjust repellent distribution schedule with their smartphones, tablets, or web browsers.

This section explains how TUDR's hardware components are integrated and how its software components are written and configured. This section also provides a guidance to reproduce TUDR.

### 1.3.1 Hardware Components

TUDR is built with the following hardware components.

- Raspberry Pi 3 Model A+ (1x): Purchase a power supply cable and a MicroSD card separately. They do not come with a Raspberry Pi computer.

- Submersible liquid pumps (2x): They are used to pump liquid repellent from a container to distribution tubes. Adafruit product ID: 4547, 4546. Amazon Standard Identification Number (ASIN): B08PBQ1N1G or B097F4576N.

- PVC tubes (2x): Purchase these if not included in liquid pumps. Adafruit product ID: 4545.

- 2-pin screw terminal blocks, 3.5mm pitch (2x): Adafruit product ID: 724. ASIN: B07QLXR1V9.

- Pimoroni Explorer HAT Pro (1x): This is required to connect a liquid pump with a Raspberry Pi. ASIN: B00WWQ20MG. Pimoroni's product Web page: [11].

- Female-to-female jumper wires (4x): These are used to wire pumps to an Explorer HAT. Adafruit product ID: 1950. ASIN: B07S2RH6Q4.

- Pimoroni Pibow 3 A+ Coupé (1x): This is an enclosure for a Raspberry Pi. It is optional, but useful to stack an Explorer HAT on a Raspberry Pi in a stable manner. ASIN: B07TWXN7ZB. Pimoroni's product Web page: [12].

ASINs can be used for product searches at `https://www.amazon.com`, and Adafruit product IDs can be used at `https://www.adafruit.com`.

### 1.3.2 Connecting an Explorer HAT to a Raspberry Pi

TUDR uses a Raspberry Pi and an Explorer HAT. HAT stands for Hardware Attached on Top, which means an add-on board that sits on a Raspberry Pi. Its backside has a GPIO connector with 40 (20x2) sockets. Stack an Explorer HAT on a Raspberry Pi by inserting GPIO pins to the GPIO connector (Fig. 4).

TUDR requires an Explorer HAT to power and control liquid pumps. Each pump is basically a DC motor that is powered with 3 to 5V and draws 100 mA. An Explorer HAT has four 5V-powered outputs, and up to 500 mA can be drawn in total from those outputs.

Note that a Raspberry Pi cannot power a pump sufficiently. 16 mA is the maximum current that can be drawn from each GPIO pin. (The total current over all pins is limited to 50 mA.)

Turn on a Raspberry Pi, and update its operating system by running the following commands on a Terminal one by one.

- `sudo apt update -y`
- `sudo apt full-upgrade -y`

Then, run the following command to make the Explorer HAT ready to be used.

- `curl https://get.pimoroni.com/explorerhat|bash`

Fig. 4: Explorer HAT stacked on a Raspberry Pi

Run the following Python program to see if the Explorer HAT is installed and configured properly.

```
import explorerhat as hat
import time

hat.light.red.on()
time.sleep(3)
hat.light.red.off()
```

A red LED (on the backside of the HAT) emits light for three seconds if the HAT is running properly.

### 1.3.3 Connecting Liquid Pumps to an Explorer HAT

Loosen the screws of a terminal block, insert two wires of a pump (red and black wires) to the terminal block, and tighten the screws (Fig. 5).

Fig. 5: Terminal Block wired with a Liquid Pump

Plug two jumper wires to the terminal block's pins. Connect the jumper wires to a 5V socket and an output socket of the Explorer HAT, as shown in Fig. 6. Make this circuit for each pump.

A 5V socket should be connect to a power (red) wire of the pump. An output socket should be connected to a ground (black) wire of the pump. This way, electrical current goes out from the 5V socket, powers the pump, and goes into the output socket. It is a bit counter-intuitive that an "output" socket sinks current, but that is how the Explorer HAT is designed to work.

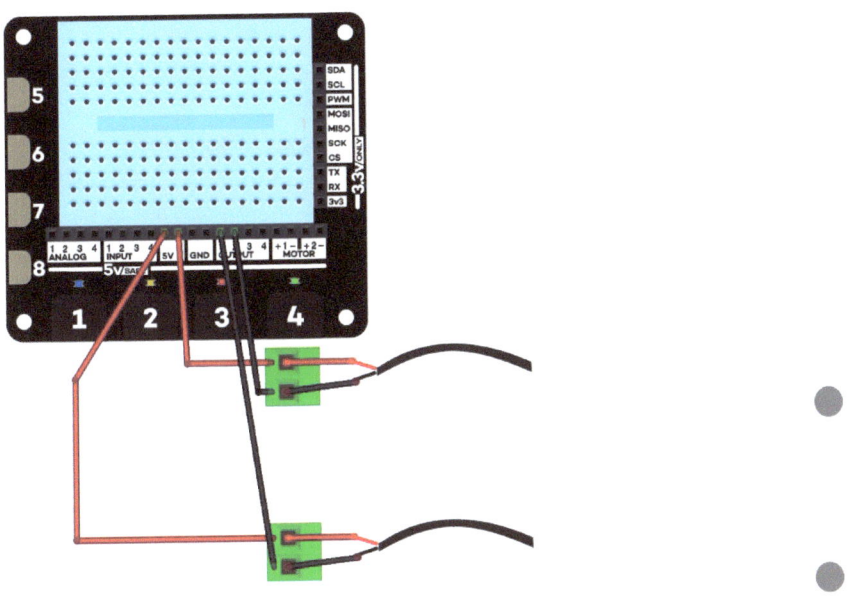

Fig. 6: Wiring of Two Pumps to an Explorer HAT

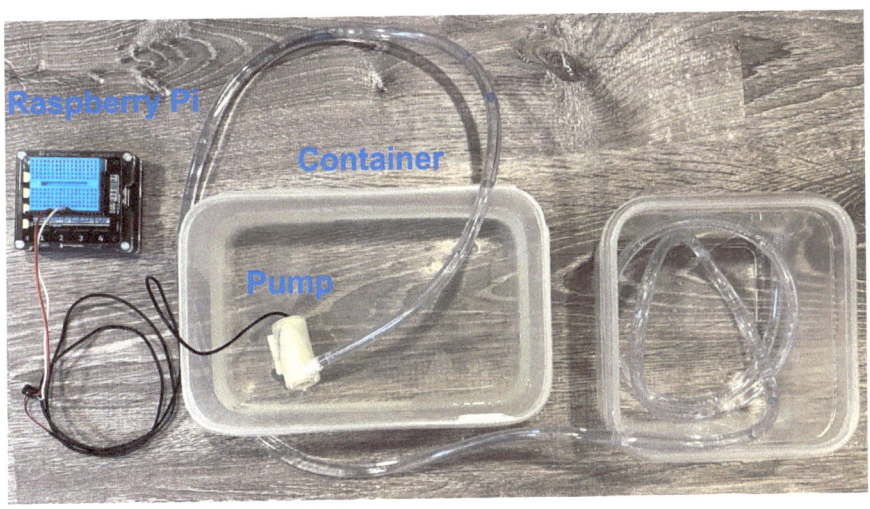

Fig. 7: Testbed for TUDR

Now, it is time to test pumps. Plug PVC tubes to the pumps. Then, put some water in a container, place the pumps in the container, and connect the tubes to an empty container (Fig. 7). Note that only one pump is shown in Fig. 7. Pumps may not work if they are not placed in water. Try not to use them without water. That will break them.

Then, run the following Python program. This turns on two pumps to suck water in from the side of the plastic casing and push it out the tubing port. They will be turned off in three seconds. In the program, `hat.output.one` and `hat.output.two` reference the first and second output sockets of the Explorer HAT.

```
import explorerhat as hat
import time

hat.output.one.on()
hat.output.two.on()
time.sleep(3)
hat.output.one.off()
hat.output.two.off()
```

By default, an output socket blocks incoming electrical current. When `on()` is called, it sinks the current. `off()` blocks the current.

After confirming that the pumps work as expected, close the end of each tube with a tube endcap. Caulk, glue and/or heat may also work to do that. Then, open small holes on tube walls with a drill.

### 1.3.4 Interacting with Kintone Cloud Database

TUDR stores the settings of repellent distribution in a cloud database called Kintone. They are stored in a database application, which is designed with several data fields as shown in Fig. 8. Those data fields are configured as follows:

- "Distribute Repellent NOW": Field type: check box. Field code: `onNow`.

- "Scheduled Repellent Distribution": Field type: check box. Field code: `weeklySchedule`.

- "Scheduled Time": Field type: check box. Field code: **onSchedule**.

- "Time": Field type: Time. Field code: **scheduledTime**.

- "Duration of Repellent Distribution (seconds)": Field type: number. Field code: **duration**.

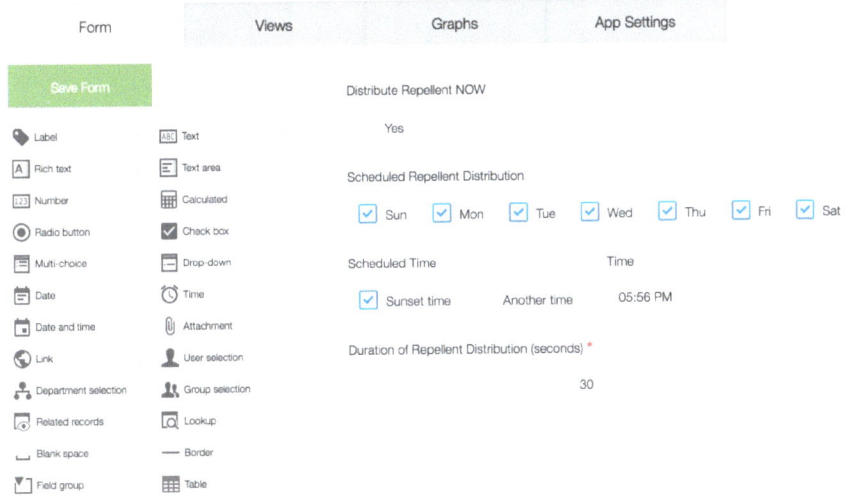

Fig. 8: Data Fields in the TUDR Kintone Application

If "Distribute Repellent NOW" is selected, TUDR will start repellent distribution within a minute. Otherwise, it follows a preset schedule. By default, it distributes repellent for 30 seconds every day at sunset.

Gardeners can remotely adjust these settings with their smartphones, tablets and web browsers. Fig. 9 shows the user interface for data entry on a smartphone.

TUDR runs a Python program on a Raspberry Pi. See the end of this section for the entire program. It contacts the TUDR Kintone application and downloads settings data every minute. Then, it turns on and off liquid pumps based on the downloaded data.

The Python program uses the built-in **datetime** module to obtain the current date and time. It also uses OpenWeatherMap, a freely-available weather data service, to obtain the sunset time of each day [13]. The `openweather` module (`openweather.py`) defines a collection of functions to use the OpenWeatherMap API. The `kintone` module (`kintone.py`) is a collection of functions to use the Kintone API. The `explorerhat` module is to use an Explorer Hat. It has been installed through a procedure in Section 1.3.2.

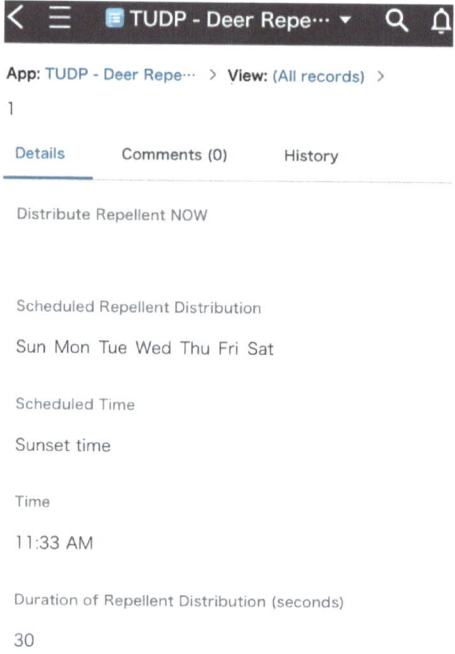

Fig. 9: Data Entry User Interface on a Smartphone

To run the TUDR Python program properly, it is required to specify the following three parameters to use OpenWeatherMap.

- Generate an API key of OpenWeatherMap and specify it in `weatherApiKey = ""`.

- Specify a zip code in `zipCode = ""`.

- Specify a country code in `countryCode = "US"`. The United States is selected by default. Change it as necessary. ISO 3166 county code is used for county code. See [14] for more details.

In addition, the Python program is required to specify the following three parameters to use Kintone.

- Specify a Kintone subdomain name in `sdomain = ""`. Enter a Kintone subdomain name in between the quotation marks.

- Specify a Kintone application ID in `appId = ""`. Enter a Kintone application ID in between the quotation marks.

- Generate a Kintone API token and specify it in `token = ""`. Enter a Kintone API token in between the quotation marks. It is a credential to call the Kintone API.

See [15] for more details about these parameter settings.

```python
from datetime import datetime
from openweather import *
import kintone, time, explorerhat as hat

weatherApiKey = ""
sdomain = ""
appId = ""
token = ""
zipCode = ""
countryCode = "US"

def turnOnPump(duration):
    hat.output.one.on()
    hat.output.two.on()
    time.sleep(duration)
    hat.output.one.off()
    hat.output.two.off()

def getWeekDay(currentDt):
    daysOfWeek = ["Mon", "Tue", "Wed", "Thu", "Fri", "Sat", "Sun"]
    return daysOfWeek[currentDt.weekday()]

while True:
    try:
        weatherData = getZipWeather(zipCode, countryCode,
                                    "imperial", weatherApiKey)
        sunsetDt = getSunsetToday(weatherData)
        sunsetHr = sunsetDt.hour
        sunsetMin = sunsetDt.minute

        currentDt = datetime.now()
        currentHr = currentDt.hour
        currentMin = currentDt.minute
        currentWkDay = getWeekDay(currentDt)

        record = kintone.getRecord(subDomain=sdomain,
```

```
                           apiToken=token,
                           appId=appId,
                           recordId="1")
        onNow = record["onNow"]["value"]
        weeklySchedule = record["weeklySchedule"]["value"]
        onSchedule = record["onSchedule"]["value"]
        scheduledTime = record["scheduledTime"]["value"]
        duration = int(record["duration"]["value"])

        if onNow == "Yes":
            turnOnPump(duration)
        elif currentWkDay in weeklySchedule:
            if "Sunset time" in onSchedule:
                if currentHr == sunsetHr and
                    currentMin == sunsetMin:
                    turnOnPump(duration)
            if "Another time" in onSchedule:
                schedTime = scheduledTime.split(":")
                schedHr = schedTime[0]
                schedMin = schedTime[1]
                if currentHr == schedHr and currentMin == schedMin:
                    turnOnPump(duration)
        time.sleep(60)
    except KeyboardInterrupt:
        break
```

## 1.4 Future Work

Several enhancements are planned for TUDR. The first enhancement is siphoning prevention (overfeeding prevention). Most inexpensive pumps do not have anti-siphon valves. As a result, if a repellent container is placed on a higher level than a tube, repellent keeps flowing into the tube even after turning off a pump. Currently, TUDR plans to use a liquid solenoid valve as an anti-siphon valve and control it between a pump and its tube.

TUDR also plans to automatically detect the remaining amount of liquid repellent in a container, so gardeners do not have to come to the container and check that out visually. The current plan is to put repellent in a tall, cylindrical container and install an ultrasonic distance sensor at the top/lid of the container. The sensor will be configured to periodically measure the distance from the lid to the liquid surface and record it in Kintone. When a refill is required (i.e., when the lid-to-surface distance becomes close to the container's height), TUDR will report it to gardeners with a messaging application.

Another plan is scaling up TUDR to extend its coverage in yards. Currently, TUDR uses a single Raspberry Pi to run two pumps. It can easily run up to four pumps because an Explorer HAT has four output sockets. However, it would require multiple Raspberry Pi computers to cover larger areas; for example, multiple yards (e.g., front and back yards) or different areas in a yard (e.g., around the front door, the garage, and the mailbox). Since it is often laborious to manage multiple computers remotely, an automation mechanism will be implemented to allow a gardener to perform multiple tasks with a single command or a single click/tap rather than doing them one by one manually. Those tasks include checking if all computers are up running normally, rebooting all computers, and terminating/re-starting Python programs on all computers.

Power efficiency is another potential enhancement. Currently, power is supplied to TUDR with an outdoor power outlet. When a Raspberry Pi needs to be placed far from the outlet, a battery would be a better choice for power supply. Therefore, a power management HAT and a real-time clock (RTC) will be tried out to automatically turn on and off a Raspberry Pi, following a preset schedule.

## 1.5 Conclusion

This chapter reports an Internet of Things (IoT) project that built a cloud-assisted, electronic deer repeller called The Ultimate Deer Repeller (TUDR). It is an outdoor, in-garden system that automatically distributes liquid repellent around garden plants. Powered by Raspberry Pi, Python and Kintone, TUDR allows gardeners to remotely set up and adjust repellent distribution schedule with smartphones, tablets, or web browsers. TUDR's Python program is available at [16].

## References

[1] J. McDonald and C. Hollingsworth, Preventing Deer Damage, Center for Agriculture, Food and the Environment, University of Massachusetts, Amherst, 2013.

[2] MassWildlife (Division of Fisheries and Wildlife, Commonwealth of Massachusetts), Living with Wildlife: White-tailed Deer in Massachusetts, MassWildlife's Web site:http://www.mass.gov/masswildlife

[3] Deer Technical Committee, Northeast Assoc. of Fish and Wildlife Agencies, An Evaluation of Deer Management Options, May 2009.

[4] MassWildlife (Division of Fisheries and Wildlife, Commonwealth of Massachusetts), Deer management: Learn how MassWildlife manages white-tailed deer statewide, MassWildlife's Web site: http://www.mass.gov/masswildlife

[5] J. Ward, Limiting Deer Browse Damage to Landscape Plants, Connecticut Agricultural Experiment Station, New Haven, Bulletin 968, November 2000.

[6] https://www.nwf.org/

[7] By User: SB_Johnny, CC BY-SA 3.0, https://commons.wikimedia.org/w/index.php?curid=1352747

[8] D. Drake, J. Paulin, P. Curtis, D. Decker, and G, San Julian, Assessment of economic impacts from deer in the northeastern United States. Journal of Extension, Volume 43, February 2005.

[9] MassWildlife (Division of Fisheries and Wildlife, Commonwealth of Massachusetts), Minimizing damage to landscaped yards and crops, MassWildlife's Web site: http://www.mass.gov/masswildlife

[10] M. Guerisoli and J. Pereira, Deer damage: A review of repellents to reduce impacts worldwide, Journal of Environmental Management, Volume 271, October 2020.

[11] https://shop.pimoroni.com/products/explorer-hat

[12] https://shop.pimoroni.com/products/pibow-3-a-plus-coupe

[13] https://openweathermap.org/

[14] https://en.wikipedia.org/wiki/List_of_ISO_3166_country_codes

[15] https://get.kintone.help/

[16] https://github.com/HSSBoston/deer-repeller/

# Biography

Hanna Suzuki is an 8th grader who loves reading, music, playing tennis, and hanging out with her friends. She is a founding organizer of AnimalHack. She has experienced coding with Lego WeDo, Scratch and Squeak Smalltalk since she was a kindergarten student. Most of her recent projects use Python and Raspberry Pi. She is a Python Certified Entry-level Programmer. Hanna has won two Global Championships (2022 and 2021) and a Global Finalist Honorable Mention (2023) in the NASA International Space Apps Challenge. She has also won the Massachusetts State Merit Award in the 3M Young Scientist Challenge in 2023. Hanna has been active to serve regional, nationwide, and international K-12 communities by sharing her skills and experience in coding and electronics. Her service was recognized by the President of the United States, and she received a Gold Medal of the President's Volunteer Service Award in 2023. Hanna also studies piano at the New England Conservatory Preparatory School and has been invited to Carnegie Hall for her recitals eight times.

# Chapter 2

# Squirrel Repeller

Shun Nagata[1] and Rei Nagata[2]

[1]Rye High School
Rye, NY 10580, USA

[2]Rye Middle School
Rye, NY 10580, USA

## Abstract

This project presents a unique solution harnessing the capabilities of a Raspberry Pi to create a smart and effective squirrel repeller. The system integrates various components to operate at its peak efficiency. For instance, there is a motorized spinning mechanism with a tiny, blunt stick attached to it to deter the animals, that is activated based on motion detection by a sensor. Meanwhile, it incorporates surveillance functionality as well, with a camera module. A Raspberry Pi is the powerhouse of the system, coordinating the roles of each component.

## 2.1 Introduction

Growing plants is a process that demands extreme precision, caution, and patience. It is one of our hobbies, but the relentless obstacles along the way are inevitable. There are varieties of obstacles, but our primary concern is keeping them intact from wild animals, especially squirrels.

In our pursuit, we attempted different methods to protect our plants, like placing a net that surrounds them. Ultimately, none of them proved to be effective. Thus, we thought it would be useful to make something to solve this perpetual problem that we were facing.

The project idea that we decided to implement was "The Squirrel Repeller." It is essentially a Raspberry Pi-powered system that scares away any wild animals that come to ruin the plants.

## 2.2 The Squirrel Repeller

Our system has a motion sensor, a camera, and a servo motor, and they are controlled by the Python code on a Raspberry Pi (Fig. 1).

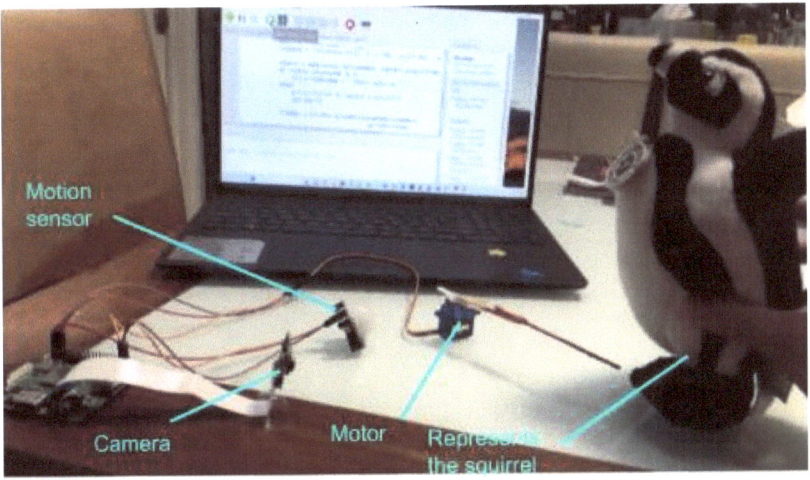

Fig. 1: The Squirrel Repeller

Upon motion detection by the sensor, the system activates the motor to drive the intruders off with the red stick attached to the end of the motor. Simultaneously, the camera takes a picture when a motion is detected. The image captured by the camera gets transferred to a designated cloud storage called Kintone (Fig. 2).

You can access your Kintone cloud storage with a Web browser or Kintone's smartphone application. As you can see in Fig. 2, the storage displays the date and time of the photo taken, along with the photo itself and a memo next to it that is labeled, "Motion detected." When clicked on the image, it gets enlarged and reveals the photo that the camera took (Fig. 3). You can zoom in even closer from there, and there is also the option to download the photo.

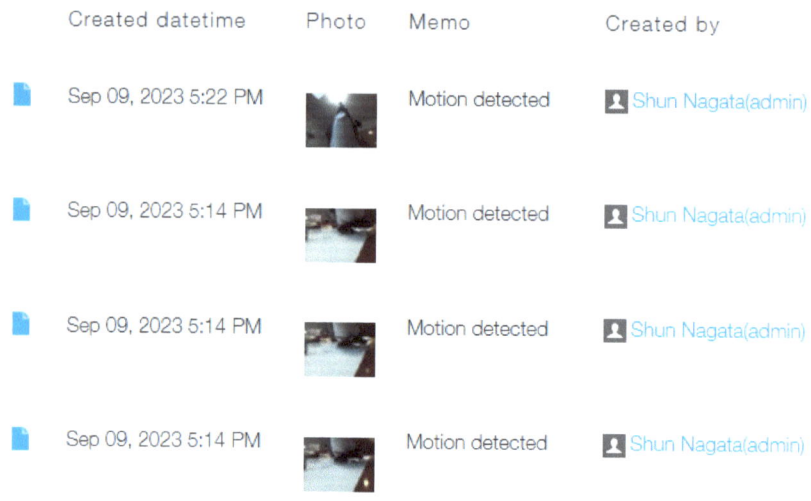

| Created datetime | Photo | Memo | Created by |
|---|---|---|---|
| Sep 09, 2023 5:22 PM | | Motion detected | Shun Nagata(admin) |
| Sep 09, 2023 5:14 PM | | Motion detected | Shun Nagata(admin) |
| Sep 09, 2023 5:14 PM | | Motion detected | Shun Nagata(admin) |
| Sep 09, 2023 5:14 PM | | Motion detected | Shun Nagata(admin) |

Fig. 2: A Series of Pictures in the Kintone Cloud Storage

Fig. 3: An Example Picture stored in Kintone

## 2.3 Use Cases

Our system is suitable for anyone who grows plants. There is no worse feeling than putting substantial time and effort into taking care of plants, only for them to be ruined by wild animals. Nonetheless, it can also be used by individuals who are seeking to use a tool to repel animals for other intentions.

Here's a potential use case. Let's say you just bought a brand-new bird feeder since you wanted to start bird watching. You hung the bird feeder on a tree in your backyard, but there was one problem; the squirrels would consistently outpace the birds. The squirrels would stand on the bird feeder and after a few days, the bird feeder succumbed and broke. Your anticipation of enjoying and cherishing this new hobby has turned into nothing but a disastrous outcome and frustration. Our system can be used to solve these problems as well.

Furthermore, the Squirrel Repeller may be customized depending on the characteristics of the animal that you want to fend off. In the case of our situation, it was the squirrel that we were repelling by spinning the red stick. Generally, the size of the tool has a direct correlation with the size of the animal. In other words, the bigger the animal is, the bigger the tool should be. For instance, smaller devices suffice for smaller animals like chipmunks and rats. On the contrary, bigger animals like coyotes require bigger instruments.

## 2.4 Hardware Setup

This section explains how you can build the Squirrel Repeller yourself. Here is a list of required parts:

- Raspberry Pi (1x): Out of the many types of Raspberry Pi models, we used Raspberry Pi 3 Model A+. It doesn't come with a power supply cable and a MicroSD card. You need to purchase them too.

- Raspberry Pi Camera Module (1x): We recommend an "official" camera module for Raspberry Pi. We used a second-generation (V2) camera module, but any generation works. Amazon Standard Identification Number (ASIN): B01ER2SKFS.

- Female-to-female jumper wires (6x): You will use them to connect a motion sensor and a servo motor to a Raspberry Pi. ASIN: B07S2RH6Q4.

- Motion sensor (1x): Use an HC-SR501 Passive InfraRed (PIR) sensor. ASIN: B0CF5514XB.

- Servo motor (1x): Use a SG90 motor. ASIN: B0BPFXTZ73.

- Wooden sticks (2x): Any kind of sticks work, but the flatter, the better. ASIN: B08XQPH3LH.

ASINs can be used for product searches at `https://www.amazon.com`, and Adafruit product IDs can be used at `https://www.adafruit.com`.

### 2.4.1 Connecting a Camera to Raspberry Pi

The first step is to connect a camera module to Raspberry Pi. Connect the camera module by pinching the middle black part of Camera Serial Interface (CSI) up and putting the tape end of the camera module as far as you can into the gap made between the black part and the white part of CSI (Fig. 4). The black plastic part is very fragile, so be careful, and don't take it out all the way!

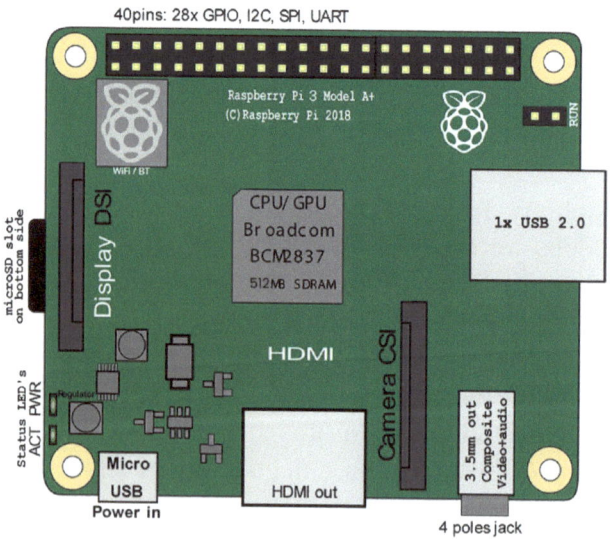

Fig. 4: Raspberry Pi 3 A+

The orientation of the camera module should have the side that has the letters written on the tape along with the camera lens towards the

3.5 mm composite (Fig. 4). After you push the camera in, you tighten the black part by pushing it down.

## 2.4.2 Connecting a Motion Sensor to Raspberry Pi

The next step is wiring the motion sensor to the Raspberry Pi. Put down the motion sensor so the orange screws are facing you, and the white semi-sphere is facing the ground. You need to turn the two orange screws counterclockwise all the way (Fig. 5).

Fig. 5: Motion Sensor Screws

Fig. 6: Motion Sensor Wiring

Now, rotate the motion sensor so the three pins face you. Take three female to female jumper wires and attach each of them to a pin on the motion sensor.

Rotate your Raspberry Pi as shown in Fig. 4. Wire your left pin to a 5V pin on the Raspberry Pi (Fig. 6). You will perform the same procedure to the middle and the right pins, but the middle goes to the GPIO 21 pin and the right goes to one of the GND pins (Fig. 6).

### 2.4.3 Connecting a Servo Motor to Raspberry Pi

Three wires come out of a servo motor, but they are intermingled at the end with a black plastic piece. Take three female to female jumper wires, one brown, one red, and one orange. Attach them to the corresponding color slots of the black piece.

Connect the red wire to the other 5V pin of your Raspberry Pi, which is right below the top right 5V pin that is already used (Fig. 7). The brown one wires with one of the GND pins, which is right below the 5V pin that you just wired. Finally, wire the orange with the GPIO 20 pin, right above the bottom right pin that you already used (Fig. 7).

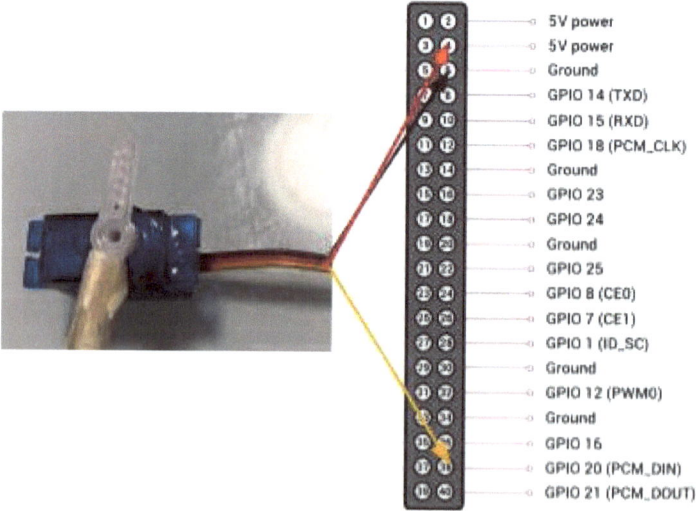

Fig. 7: Servo Motor Wiring

### 2.4.4 Final Setup

You are also going to make a miniature wooden tool. You can design it yourself if you'd prefer. Our method was to combine two flat sticks with a slanted edge pointing away. You can use as many sticks as you want of any type, but one tip while making the device is to take into account the air resistance. The flatter it is, the less air resistance it receives, therefore making it more mobile. After you finish making the instrument, you will link it to the propellers of the servo motor.

Now, arrange the locations of the hardware components, the camera lens facing the right direction, and the motor propeller being in range to deter animals (Fig. 8).

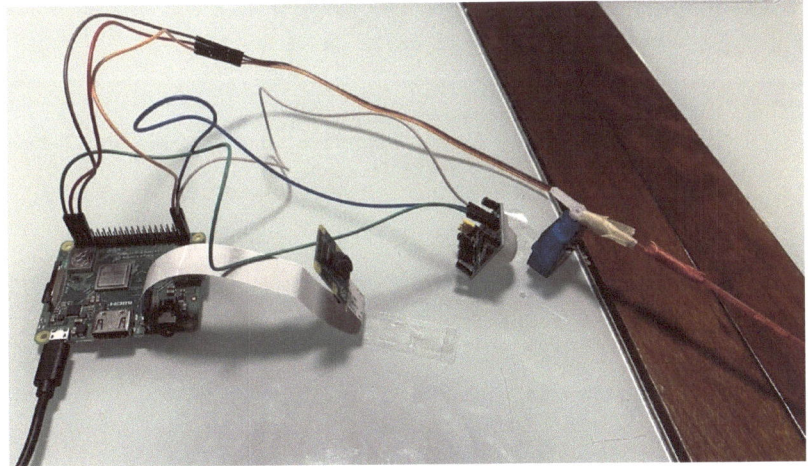

Fig. 8: Completed Setup

## 2.5 Coding

The code we wrote for this project is shown below.

```
import RPi.GPIO as GPIO
import time, iotutils, subprocess, sys, kintone
from iotutils import getCurrentTimeStamp
GPIO.setmode(GPIO.BCM)

sdomain = ""
appId = ""
token = ""
```

```
servo_pin = 20
motion_sensor_pin = 21
GPIO.setup(servo_pin, GPIO.OUT)
GPIO.setup(motion_sensor_pin, GPIO.IN)

pwm = GPIO.PWM(servo_pin, 50)
pwm.start(0)

try:
    while True:
        motion_detected = GPIO.input(motion_sensor_pin)

        if motion_detected:
            for duty_cycle in range(0, 13):
                pwm.ChangeDutyCycle(duty_cycle)
                time.sleep(0.02)
            print("Motion detected: ", end="")

            timeStamp = getCurrentTimeStamp()
            picFile = timeStamp + ".jpg"
            command = "libcamera-still -n -t 500"
                        + "--width 800 --height 600 -o "
                        + picFile
            status = subprocess.run(command,
                                    capture_output=True, shell=True)
            if status.returncode == 0:
                print(timeStamp + " Photo captured.")
            else:
                print("Failed to capture a picture")
                sys.exit()

            fileKey = kintone.uploadFile(subDomain=sdomain,
                                         apiToken=token,
                                         filePath=picFile)
            if fileKey is None:
                sys.exit()

            memo = "Motion detected"
            payload = {
                "app": appId,
                "record": {"photo": {
                            "value": [{"fileKey": fileKey}]},
                            "memo": {"value": memo} }}
            recordId = kintone.uploadRecord(subDomain=sdomain,
                                            apiToken=token,
                                            record=payload)
            if recordId is None:
                sys.exit()

except KeyboardInterrupt:
    pwm.stop()
    GPIO.cleanup()
```

You need to edit Lines 6 to 8 in red based on your Kintone settings.
In Line 6: sdomain = "", enter the name of your Kintone subdomain

in between the quotation marks. If your Kintone application runs at `https://abc.kintone.com/.../`, your subdomain is `abc`.

In Line 7: `appId = ""`, enter the ID of your Kintone application in between the quotation marks. If your Kintone application runs at `https://abc.kintone.com/k/1/`, your application's ID is 1.

In Line 8: `token = ""`, type in your Kintone API token in between the quotation marks. It is a credential for the Squirrel Repeller to use Kintone. See `https://get.kintone.help/` regarding how to generate an API token in your Kintone application.

In Lines 24 and 26, "13" in `range(0, 13)` and "0.02" in `time.sleep(0.02)` determine the servo motor's range and frequency. By modifying these numbers, we found this is the best combination for us. You can vary them as you like.

Congratulations! You have completed the Squirrel Repeller. Run the code and test out the system to see if it works as you expect.

## 2.6 Future Steps

We have a few plans to improve the Squirrel Repeller. First, we plan to use a bigger servo motor to get more range, which makes it more effective for repelling wild animals. We also want to make the wooden stick attached to the motor sturdier.

In addition to spinning a stick, we will consider to implement extra repelling options in our system, such as making intimidating sounds and emitting odors that the animals despise.

Another plan is to use the Squirrel Repeller as a live surveillance system for our home garden. Through a stream of pictures, it would be able to answer various questions; for example: which wildlife species approach garden plants, how big/small they are, and how they eat and damage garden plants.

It would be possible to perform data analysis with the dataset our system collects. It could reveal some patterns of wild animals approaching garden plants, such as what time frames they are active/inactive and how often they approach plants.

## 2.7 Conclusion

AnimalHack 2023 was our first experience to participate in an international hackathon. We encountered a number of challenges that required us to think hard, make careful decisions, and troubleshoot by trial and error. Every step, from inception to completion, involved much deliberation, gathering materials, and creation.

It was a challenge to figure out which GPIO pins to use for connecting a servo motor to Raspberry Pi. You must use specific pins as elaborated in Section 4. We needed to reference various Web sites to figure this out. Another hurdle that we faced was coding. It was by far the most complex and time-consuming step in this project. For example, we needed to spend a lot of time figuring out how to upload a photo to Kintone. Despite these challenges, we managed to complete this project. We hope you will find success and enjoyment in accomplishing this project!

## Biography

Shun Nagata is a sports enthusiast who loves data analytics and coding. Currently a 10th grader, Shun is a starting center-midfielder in the varsity soccer team while playing on a club team. He has won a few championships in regional and national leagues/tournaments. He is also a JV baseball player. Shun has a strong interest in data analytics, especially sabermetrics. He studies various baseball stats and practices them in fantasy baseball leagues. He even developed a new stat category of his own and has been analyzing it with real game datasets. Shun exercises his Python coding skill to implement the baseball stats and build Internet of Things devices. He won the Silver Prize at AnimalHack 2023.

Rei Nagata is a serious 8th-grade soccer player who loves animals. He plays on a club team in the Major League Soccer NEXT league, which is the highest-level competition platform in the US and Canada. He plays against professional academy teams such as NYCFC. He also enjoys playing baseball as a pitcher and an outfielder. Rei is a life-long animal lover, feeding birds and keeping dogs, frogs and even mantis at home. He has a strong interest in coding and learns about Python through online courses offered by University of Michigan. He won the Silver Prize at AnimalHack 2023.

# Chapter 3

# Hydrate Cat

Yuma Karube

Tesla STEM High School
Redmond, WA 98053, USA

## Abstract

This project builds a hydration monitor for domestic cats. Using a Raspberry Pi computer and its peripherals such as a weight sensor, this product monitors the amount of water a cat consumes throughout the day, records the water consumption in a cloud data storage, and visualizes the time-series consumption data as graphs. It is intended to provide cat owners with data-driven insights on whether their cats stay hydrated well. Its ultimate goal is to help them promote their cats' health and wellbeing.

## 3.1 Introduction

Hydration is a key health factor for domestic cats. Proper hydration can prevent common health issues such as urinary tract infections and kidney disease. It is especially critical for senior cats, nursing cats, cats with chronic conditions, and cats eating dry food primarily, because they are very prone to dehydration. Therefore, it is important to give cats access to fresh water at all times.

However, it is challenging to ensure that cats stay hydrated well – neither too little nor too much. Since they are often independent, more independent than other pets, it is not that common to visually catch them sipping. They do not communicate with their owners about their thirsts, of course.

To solve this problem, I developed "Hydrate Cat," which is a hydration monitor for cats (Fig. 1). This device monitors, records and visualizes the amount of water a cat consumes throughout the day by tracking its weight changes. It is designed to help pet owners understand whether their cats maintain a healthy range of daily water consumption and help them take interventions as necessary, such as feeding wet food, improving water quality, offering multiple water stations, and using flowing water rather than a stationary bowl.

Fig. 1: Hydrate Cat, placed under a Water Bowl

## 3.2 An Overview of Hydrate Cat

Hydrate Cat is built with a Raspberry Pi single-board computer and its peripheral devices. Python code runs on it to operate a weight sensor under a water bowl and keep track of the bowl's weight every minute (Figs. 1 and 2). It determines water consumption by observing a 10-gram decrease in the weight, considering the average of the three measurements before and after. As a reference, according to `Cat-World.com`, the daily water requirement for a cat is generally around 8 fluid ounces or approximately 240 grams.

The Python code sends all collected data to a cloud service known as Kintone. In Kintone, I have implemented a system that records each time the cat drinks water. It displays the date and time when the data was collected and sometimes includes a text labeled "Cat Hydrated!" (Fig. 3). This indicates that Hydrate Cat has detected water consumption (a 10-gram decrease in the water bowl's weight).

Fig. 2: Cat, about to Sip Water

| Record number | Date and time | Number | Date | Text | | |
|---|---|---|---|---|---|---|
| 19203 | Sep 08, 2023 11:05 PM | 2038.51 | 2023-09-08-23-05-08 | | / | O |
| 19202 | Sep 08, 2023 11:05 PM | 2038.47 | 2023-09-08-23-05-01 | | / | O |
| 19201 | Sep 08, 2023 11:04 PM | 2038.55 | 2023-09-08-23-04-54 | | / | O |
| 19200 | Sep 08, 2023 11:04 PM | 2038.56 | 2023-09-08-23-04-46 | Cat Hydrated! | / | O |
| 19199 | Sep 08, 2023 11:04 PM | 2090.16 | 2023-09-08-23-04-39 | Cat Hydrated! | / | O |
| 19198 | Sep 08, 2023 11:04 PM | 2206.58 | 2023-09-08-23-04-32 | | / | O |
| 19197 | Sep 08, 2023 11:04 PM | 2062.75 | 2023-09-08-23-04-25 | | / | O |
| 19196 | Sep 08, 2023 11:04 PM | 2062.76 | 2023-09-08-23-04-17 | | / | O |

Fig. 3: Water Consumption Data in Kintone

## 3.3 Building Hydrate Cat

This section explains how to build Hydrate Cat.

### 3.3.1 Hardware Components

Hydrate Cat requires the following hardware components.

- Raspberry Pi Zero 2W: Used for running Python programs. Also, you must purchase a power supply cable and a MicroSD card separately as they are not included with the Raspberry Pi.

- MakerHawk Digital Load Cell Weight Sensor HX711 AD Converter Breakout Module 5KG Portable Electronic Kitchen Scale for Arduino: This package includes both a weight sensor and an analog-to-digital (AD) converter, which are already wired and ready to be used.

- UCTRONICS 0.96 Inch OLED Module 12864 128x64: Used to display the weight of a water bowl.

- Breadboard: Used for wiring the OLED and Raspberry Pi. Any size will work fine.

- Container: Used optionally to place and stabilize a water bowl.

- Female-to-female jumper wires (4x): Used for connecting hardware components to a Raspberry Pi.

- Male-to-female jumper wires (4x): Used for connecting hardware components to a Raspberry Pi.

### 3.3.2 Wiring an OLED Module

In this step, you will connect an OLED module to your Raspberry Pi with jumper wires and a breadboard. You will use the following components:

- Raspberry Pi
- OLED Module
- Male-to-female jumper wires (4x)
- Breadboard

First, take the OLED module and connect the metal tip to the breadboard as shown in Fig. 4. Then, use the male-to-female jumper wires to wire them as follows:

- Raspberry Pi's GPIO 21 pin to OLED module's VCC
- Raspberry Pi's GPIO 20 pin to OLED module's SDA
- Raspberry Pi's GPIO 16 pin to OLED module's SCL
- Raspberry Pi's GND pin to OLED module's GND

Fig. 4 shows these wiring connections.

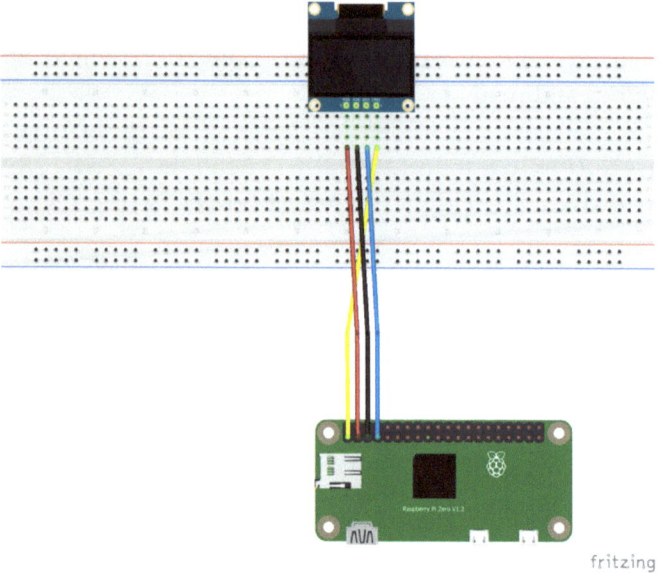

Fig. 4: Wiring of an OLED Module to a Raspberry Pi

### 3.3.3 Wiring a Weight Sensor

In this step, you will connect a weight sensor to your Raspberry Pi with jumper wires. You will use the following hardware components:

- Raspberry Pi
- Weight sensor
- Female-to-female jumper wires (4x)

Then, connect them with female-to-female jumper wires, as follows:

- Raspberry Pi's 5V pin to weight sensor's VCC
- Raspberry Pi's GND pin to weight sensor's GND
- Raspberry Pi's GPIO 5 pin to weight sensor's DT

- Raspberry Pi's GPIO 6 pin to weight sensor's SCK

This wiring is shown in Fig. 5. The weight sensor and its AD converter are wired when they are shipped.

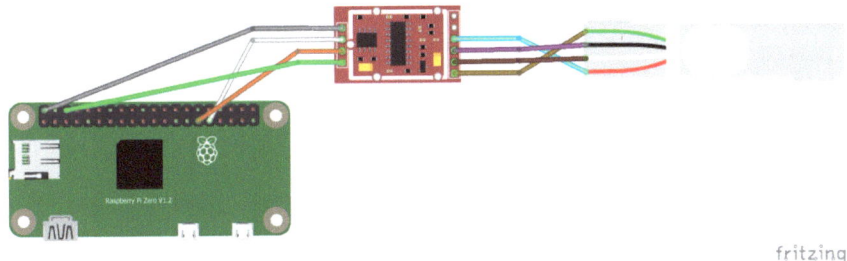

Fig 5: Wiring of a Weight Sensor to a Raspberry Pi

Here is the final setup for the project (Fig. 6). The weight sensor should already be prepared for placing water fountains, but if it doesn't seem stable, attach the container on top of the weight sensor to stabilize it.

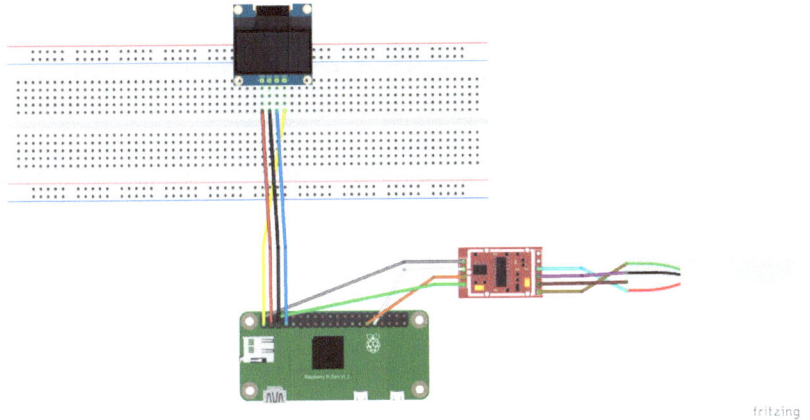

Fig. 6: Final Setup

## 3.4 Python Code for Hydrate Cat

Hydrate Cat runs Python code on a Raspberry Pi to operate a weight sensor under a water bowl and keep track of the bowl's weight every minute. The Python code is shown below.

```python
import time, subprocess, sys, time, kintone, iotutils
from iotutils import getCurrentTimeStamp
import adafruitSSD1306, RPi.GPIO as GPIO
from hx711 import HX711
from PIL import Image, ImageDraw, ImageFont

interval = 60

# kintone setup
sdomain = ""
appId = ""
token = ""

# SSD1306 (OLED) setup
font = ImageFont.truetype('SourceHanSansJP-Medium.otf', 16)
disp = adafruitSSD1306.initialize_display()
image, draw = adafruitSSD1306.initialize_image(disp)

# Show warning message during startup
adafruitSSD1306.write_image(disp, draw, image, font,
                            "** Not Ready **", "Don't put",
                            "Anything.")

try:
    GPIO.setmode(GPIO.BCM)

    # HX711 (scale) setup
    hx = HX711(dout_pin=5, pd_sck_pin=6)
    err = hx.zero()
    if err:
        adafruitSSD1306.write_image(disp, draw, image, font,
                                    "", "Tare is unsuccessful.", "")
        raise ValueError('Tare is unsuccessful.')

    # Adjusting scale ratio
    #hx.set_scale_ratio(442.15296367112813)
    hx.set_scale_ratio(442.7005649717514)

    weights = []

    while True:
        # reading weight
        reading = round(float(hx.get_weight_mean(20)), 2)

        if reading == 0:
            print("Reading value is 0. Meansuring again.")
            continue

        myMessage = ""

        if len(weights) < 6:
            weights.append(reading)
        elif len(weights) == 6:
            del weights[0]
            weights.append(reading)
            if (sum(weights[3:5]) - sum(weights[0:2])) > 10:
                myMessage = "Cat Hydrated!"

        # Uploading Data to Kintone
        date = getCurrentTimeStamp()
```

```
        number = reading
        payload = {"app": appId,
                    "record": {"number": {"value": number },
                                "date": {"value": date },
                                "text": {"value": myMessage} }}

        recordId = kintone.uploadRecord(subDomain=sdomain,
                                            apiToken=token,
                                            record=payload)

        if recordId is None:
            sys.exit()

        print(reading, 'g')
        adafruitSSD1306.write_image(disp, draw, image, font,
                                    "", str(reading) + " gram", "")

        time.sleep(interval)
except (KeyboardInterrupt, SystemExit):
    adafruitSSD1306.write_image(disp, draw, image, font,
                                "", "Bye", "")
    print('Bye :)')

finally:
    GPIO.cleanup()
```

In the three lines in red, you need to specify parameters to use Kintone. Specify your Kintone subdomain name as "sdomain," a Kintone application ID as "appId," and a Kintone API token as "token."

## 3.5 Visualizing Water Consumption Data

Hydrate Cat visualizes the temporal weight changes of a water bowl as graphs, so cat owners can intuitively understand how often and how much their cats consume water.

Hydrate Cat extracts the timestamps stored in Kintone and converts them to Unix seconds, which is the number of seconds since the beginning of the Unix epoch (i.e., 0:00 AM on January 1, 1970, in UTC). This conversion is carried out with the following code.

```
import sys, re, csv, pprint, datetime

csvFile = sys.argv[1]
minOfData = 1550

with open(csvFile) as f:
    reader = csv.reader(f)
    for row in reader:
        dataCSV = re.split('/|\s+|:', row[0])
        # ['07', '02', '2023', '21', '36']
        dataDate = datetime.datetime(int(dataCSV[2]), int(dataCSV[0]),
                                    int(dataCSV[1]), int(dataCSV[3]),
```

```
                                      int(dataCSV[4]))
      dataEpoch = dataDate.timestamp()
      if float(row[1]) < minOfData:
          continue
      else:
          print(str(dataEpoch) + " " + row[1])
```

Hydrate Cat generates a graph with the following code.

```
import sys, re, numpy as np
import matplotlib.pyplot as plt

dataFile = sys.argv[1]
xLabel = 'seconds'
yLabel = 'gram'

x = np.array([])
y = np.array([])

with open(dataFile) as f:
    for s_line in f:
        data = s_line.split()
        x = np.append(x, float(data[0]))
        y = np.append(y, float(data[1]))

plt.scatter(x, y, color="k", s=5)
plt.xlabel(xLabel)
plt.ylabel(yLabel)
plt.show()
```

Figs. 7 and 8 show how the weight of a water bowl changes over time during two particular periods of a day. The data below 1500 grams are excluded from the dataset.

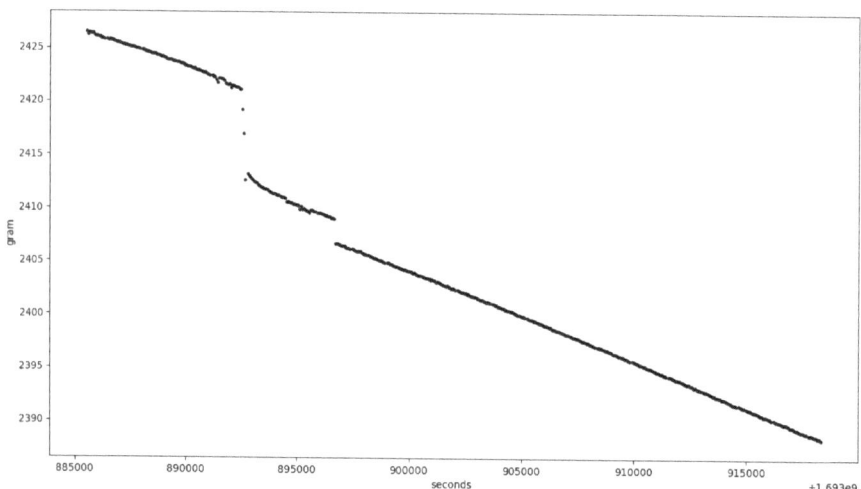

Fig. 7: Changes in the Weight of a Water Bowl (1)

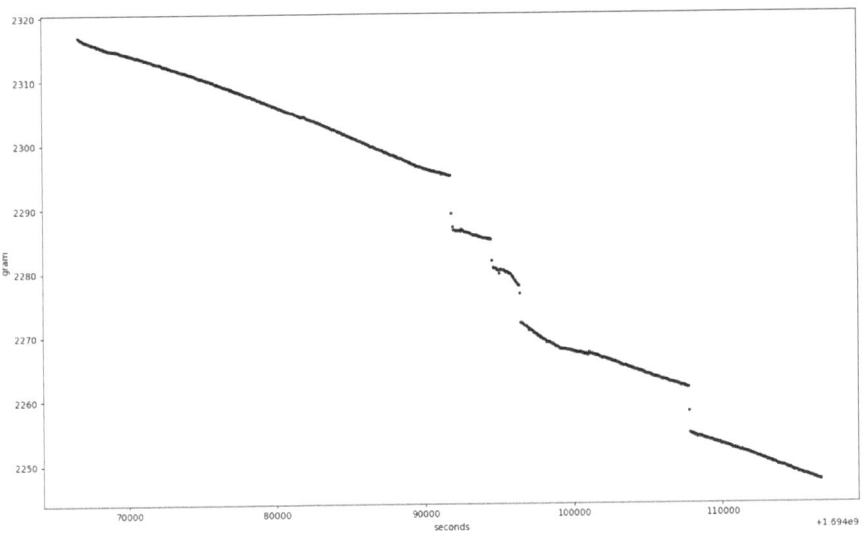

Fig. 8: Changes in the Weight of a Water Bowl (2)

In each graph, the X-axis indicates time in seconds and the Y-axis indicates weight in grams. In most of the time, water weight decreases continuously, semi-linearly, due to evaporation. It drops when a cat consumes water. For example, Fig. 7 shows a rapid 10-gram drop in three minutes, which indicates water consumption by a cat. Fig. 8 shows four consecutive 15-gram drops, which implies a cat was thirsty and consumed a relatively large amount of water.

## 3.6 Future Work

A few improvements are planned for Hydrate Cat. The first plan is to implement a notification system designed to provide alerts specifically when the cat consumes water. This will help pet owners better maintain their cat's health by keeping them consistently informed about their cat's hydration habits, rather than simply ignoring them.

Hydrate Cat has plans to improve the process of determining water consumption for cats. Currently, Kintone determines water consumption by observing a 10g decrease in weight through the weight sensor. However, this method might not be very accurate since the cat might drink at a slower pace. To solve this issue, Hydrate Cat plans to find the rate of water evaporation. By comparing the speed at which the weight drops to the expected evaporation rate, Kintone might be able to determine water consumption with greater accuracy.

Another plan the Hydrate Cat has is to implement machine-learning algorithms to analyze patterns of the cat's behavior in water consumption. This also helps better maintain cat health for pet owners by better understanding their cat's hydration habits and recognizing the differences in cat's behavior.

## 3.7 Conclusion

Hydrate Cat enhances traditional water bowls for cats by integrating them with a Raspberry Pi and its peripherals such as a weight sensor and an OLED display. It provides pet owners with data-driven insights on whether their cats stay well-hydrated by monitoring the amount of water their cats consume, recording the water consumption in a cloud data storage and visualizing the time-series consumption data as graphs. Hydrate Cat is designed to help pet owners promote their cats' health and wellbeing.

## Biography

Yuma Karube is a 10th-grader who likes to read books and play video games. He co-founded AnimalHack and co-chaired its inaugural edition in 2023. By immersing himself in the world of the Internet of Things and teaching K-12 students Python programming and electrical engineering, he regularly develops his skills in Python and leadership. He even got his service recognized by the President of the United States and received a Gold Medal on the President's Volunteer Service Award in 2023. He is passionate about learning more about computer science because of how interesting and how it can be applied to a wide range of problems. Yuma has been actively going to one of the best STEM high schools in the nation and is a Certified Entry-Level Python Programmer.

# Chapter 4

# Pet Picker: Criteria Search for Suitable Pets

Soham Vij

svij024@gmail.com

## Abstract

Pet Picker is a unique website built to provide users with pets compatible with their preferences which are entered through an easy-to-understand control panel. Users can input the metrics of their preferred qualities including maintenance, social level, life span, and vegan diet compatibility. Appropriate pets that fit the specified requirements of the user will be shown on screen, alongside some basic info and a link for the user to do more research on their own. It supports screen dimensions of all sizes and is mobile-friendly. It contains accurate data on 25+ pets, with more to come.

## 4.1 Introduction

Owning a pet is quite often an important responsibility, far from a mere casual whim. According to the Human Animal Bond Research Institute (`https://habri.org/`), 83% of pet owners report dedicating considerable daily time to their companions. Pets also tend to be a financial commitment too, with a typical dog costing $22,000 to $55,000 over its lifetime. Pets need to be loved, fed, and taken care of, often over a span of 10-15 years. Given these considerations, choosing the right pet is crucial.

Personally, my family and I have considered buying a pet on multiple occasions. What has always prevented us from getting one though, is the process of finding the right one. In general, there is a lack of high-quality resources for finding pets. I can imagine this difficulty prevents other families from adopting pets as well. According to the American Society for the Prevention of Cruelty to Animals (`https://www.aspca.org/`), over 920,000 shelter animals are euthanized each year due to factors like overcrowding. With an easier way to research potential pets, it's possible more families will be inclined to adopt, bringing this number down. This service is exactly what Pet Picker is intended to provide.

## 4.2 Wireframing

Pet Picker's initial concept (Fig. 1), which is fairly accurate to the final version, was a simple input section to the left of a grid containing pet cards with minimal info on pets that match the criteria specified in the input section. The criteria that users would input included maintenance, social level, life span, and price per month.

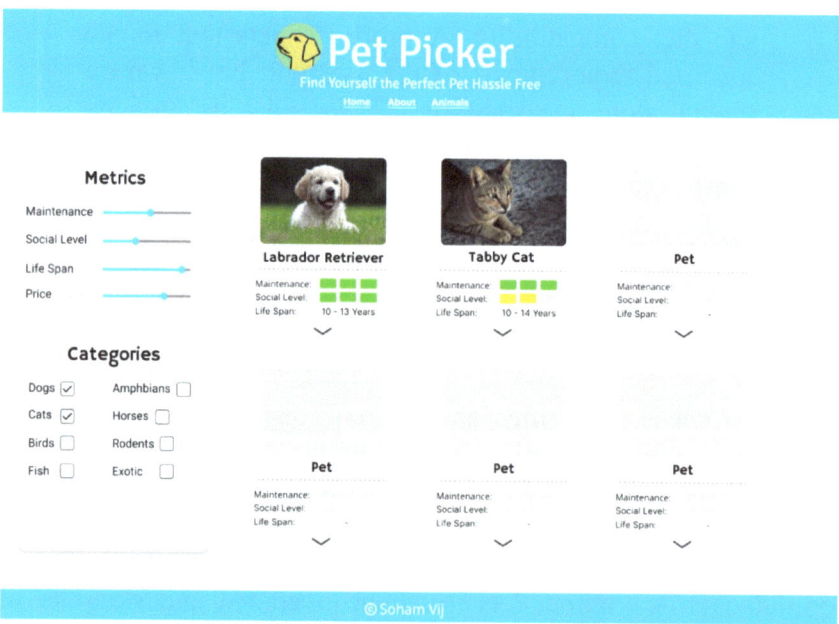

Fig. 1: Pet Picker Initial Concept designed in Figma

I designed a wireframe and decorated it in Figma, an online UI design tool. This proved to be useful when replicating the design in CSS, since there is a Figma plugin for Visual Studio Code (the primary IDE for this project) which displays recommended rule sets for different aspects of the layout. I also designed two more pages for the site: An about page containing FAQ, credits, and contact info, and an info page for information about an animal (Fig. 2). The idea with the info page was to make one for each animal, and link to that page in the corresponding pet card that would be shown in the grid in Fig. 1. This as of yet has not been built due to the sheer amount of effort required to make over 25 custom pages for animals, and as a replacement I have simply linked to the animals Wikipedia page.

Fig. 2: Pet Info Page Wireframe

## 4.3 Production and Obstacles

For the most part, replicating these designs in HTML and CSS went smooth with little to note. I refrained from using any templates or libraries for the design of site, for a couple reasons: I wanted to see what I was capable of creating with plain HTML and CSS, and I wanted to learn how to solve problems and accomplish goals myself, without external aid. This did force me to get creative in some situations though. For instance, I wanted to include a tooltip next to each range slider in the input section as seen in Fig. 3.

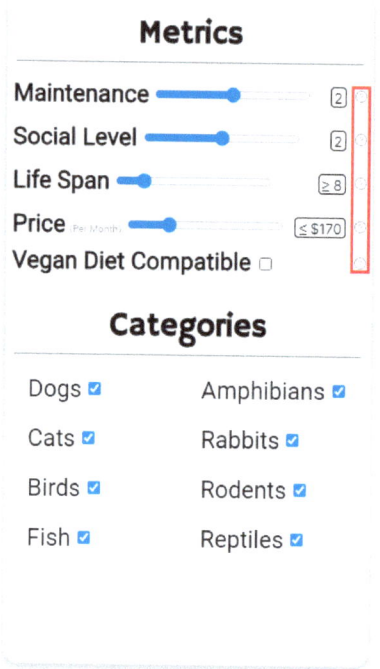

Fig. 3: Input Section with Tooltips

The first thought that popped into my head was a hover pseudo-class that would display text when the tooltip was hovered up. Upon further thought I recognized this wouldn't be optimal: I would need to have some hidden text positioned near the link that would be shown on hover, but even still this would still look odd since it wouldn't be guaranteed that the text would appear next to the cursor, since its location would be static but the mouse's location could be anywhere on the link.

The effect I intended to achieve was similar to what's seen on Wikipedia when you hover over a link (Fig. 4), a pop-up with detailed provided.

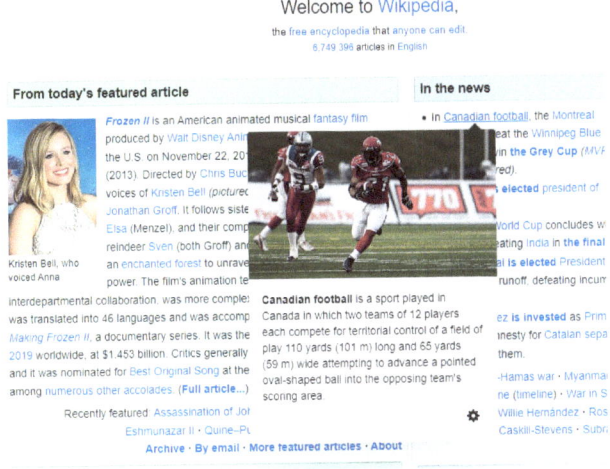

Fig. 4: Wikipedia Link-info Effect

The solution I came up with was rather simple. If you are familiar with HTML, you may recall a title attribute for anchor elements. This is typically used with links, to provide some text detailing where that link will lead. Here, I wrapped an image in an anchor tag with a title attribute displaying the text of the tooltip and the href attribute leading nowhere.

```
<a href="#" class="tooltip" title="Average lifetime of pet in years"><img
    src="resources/images/help.svg"></a>
```

The effect is exactly how I intended it to look. The result is below.

Another area of focus for this project was for it to be friendly with screens of all sizes, making it mobile, tablet, and PC friendly. I intended to do this via CSS media queries. Media queries allow for screen size-dependent rulesets, altering how elements look based on pixel width and length. One place in need of this was the animal grid right of the input section, which would collide with the input section and be pushed off screen on smaller screens (Fig. 5).

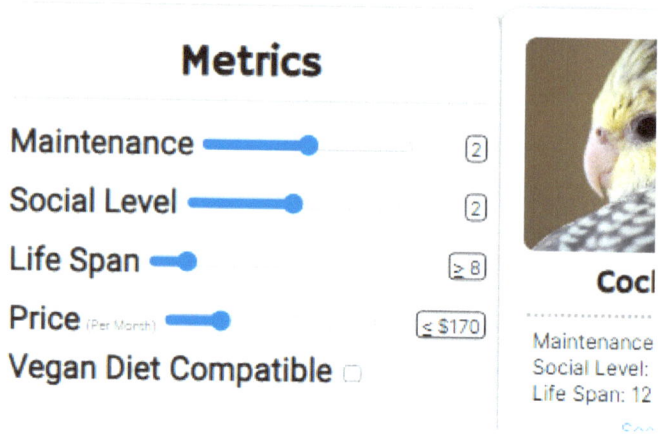

Fig. 5: Cramped Display on Smaller Screens

```
main {
    display: flex;
    flex: 1;
}
```

Here, the solution was a little more involved than just a simple media query, as my intentions were to refactor the pet grid under the input section rather than to the right of it. Achieving this took a few steps. First I configured the entirety of the main element to be a flexbox as seen in above. Main contained exactly 2 elements, a division element containing the pet grid, and a division element containing the input section. Next I created a media query to change the direction of the flexbox from row (default) to column. This would effectively modify the pet grid and input section from being side by side to stacked on top of each other.

```
@media only screen and (max-width: 640px) {
    main {
        flex-direction: column;
        align-items: center;
    }
}
```

The final few steps were to configure the amount of columns on various screen sizes, but these configurations are of little interest. Media queries were used in various aspects of the project: they are used in the header of the page, the side bars of the about page, and the elements of the input section, just to name a few.

The more interesting aspect of this project would be the JavaScript. Simply put, the job of the JavaScript is to take user inputs from the checkboxes and range sliders and accordingly display appropriate pets. To accomplish this, I needed some way for the JavaScript to access the data on the pets for it to compare against user input. This data was provided via an array of pets made from a class with fields to contain data for that pet.

```javascript
class Pet {
    constructor(name, type, maintenance, socialLevel, lifeSpan, price, veganCompat) {
        this._name = name;
        this._type = type;
        this._maintenance = maintenance;
        this._socialLevel = socialLevel;
        this._lifeSpan = lifeSpan;
        this._price = price;
        this._veganCompat = veganCompat;
    }

    get name() {
        return this._name;
    }

    get type() {
        return this._type;
    }

    get maintenance() {
        return this._maintenance;
    }

    get socialLevel() {
        return this._socialLevel;
    }

    get lifeSpan() {
        return this._lifeSpan;
    }

    get price() {
        return this._price;
    }

    get veganCompat() {
        return this._veganCompat;
    }
```

```
let pets = [new Pet('labradorRetriever', 'dog', 3, 3, 12, 155, true),
new Pet('goldfish', 'fish', 2, 1, 10, 20, true),
new Pet('siameseCat', 'cat', 2, 3, 17.5, 55, false),
new Pet('bettaFish', 'fish', 1, 2, 3, 12, false),
new Pet('cockatiel', 'bird', 2, 2, 13.5, 40, true),
new Pet('hamster', 'rodent', 1, 2, 3, 15, true),
new Pet('chameleon', 'reptile', 3, 1, 6, 42, false),
new Pet('chihuahua', 'dog', 1, 2, 13, 90, true),
new Pet('miniatureLop', 'rabbit', 2, 3, 10, 55, true),
new Pet('easternNewt', 'amphibian', 2, 1, 14, 30, false),
new Pet('guineaPig', 'rodent', 2, 3, 6, 40, true),
new Pet('persianCat', 'cat', 3, 2, 14, 320, false),
new Pet('russianTortoise', 'reptile', 1, 1, 47, 70, true),
new Pet('greyParrot', 'bird', 3, 3, 54, 470, true),
new Pet('pacmanFrog', 'amphibian', 2, 1, 12, 25, false),
new Pet('siberianHusky', 'dog', 3, 3, 14, 170, true),
new Pet('beardedDragon', 'reptile', 2, 1, 9, 80, false),
new Pet('beagle', 'dog', 2, 3, 14, 123, true),
new Pet('jerseyWooly', 'rabbit', 1, 2, 9, 50, true),
new Pet('pomeranian', 'dog', 2, 2, 14, 120, true),
new Pet('fancyRat', 'rodent', 1, 3, 3, 22, true),
new Pet('budgerigar', 'bird', 1, 3, 8, 32, true),
new Pet('italianGreyhound', 'dog', 1, 3, 14, 120, true),
new Pet('scottishFold', 'cat', 1, 3, 13, 115, false),
new Pet('cornSnake', 'reptile', 1, 1, 12, 40, false),
new Pet('dwarfFrog', 'reptile', 1, 1, 6, 28, false)
];
```

Next, I created two more arrays to store references to the various input elements on the page.

```
let sliders = [document.getElementById('maintenance-slider'), document.getElementById('social-level-slider'), documen

let checkboxes = [document.getElementById('vegan-checkbox'), document.getElementById('dogs-checkbox'), document.getEl
document.getElementById('fish-checkbox'), document.getElementById('amphibians-checkbox'), document.getElementById('ra
document.getElementById('reptiles-checkbox')];
```

But now it was time for the function which determines which pet should be displayed based on what the user entered. Conceptualizing how I was going to write this method was a challenge. I went through multiple iterations, attempting to optimize the algorithm, most of them failing. I eventually settled for this:

```
function inputChange(event) {
    pets.forEach(pet => {
        if (pet.maintenance <= parseFloat(sliders[0].value) &&
            pet.socialLevel === parseFloat(sliders[1].value) &&
            pet.lifeSpan >= parseFloat(sliders[2].value) &&
            pet.price <= parseFloat(sliders[3].value) &&
            (!checkboxes[0].checked || checkboxes[0].checked && pet.veganCompat) &&
            pet.categoryShown()) document.getElementById(pet.name).style.display = 'flex';
        else document.getElementById(pet.name).style.display = 'none';
    })
}
```

Here, the maintenance, social level, lifespan, and price is compared against the value given by a user upon an input. For the following line of code:

```
!checkboxes[0].checked || checkboxes[0].checked && pet.veganCompat
```

`checkboxes[0]` refers to a checkbox which checked, indicates that only pets that are compatible with vegan diets should be shown, and if unchecked, is completely irrelevant to the algorithm. Thus, `!checkboxes[0].checked` checks if the checkbox is not checked, in which case the algorithm continues, while `checkboxes[0].checked && pet.veganCompat` checks for if the checkbox is checked and the pet is vegan diet compatible, in which case the animal passes this check and the next and final check, which calls a method of the pets class to check whether or not the pets category is shown. The method that it calls takes the pets type (dog, bird, cat, etc.) and checks if the corresponding checkbox is checked. If the pet passes all of these checks, then and only then is it shown.

There was also a wide array of non-programming problems I encountered as well. For one, the 1-3 scale for maintenance and social interaction I used had drawbacks. These metrics, when scored relative to all pets, can result in nearly identical scores within some pet categories. For instance, all fish would score 1 for social level and maintenance in comparison to dogs. This is not valuable information. If the user wanted to get a fish that was more social than average (for a fish of course) they wouldn't be able to determine which fish to adopt since they would all have a social level of one.

My solution to this was assigning maintenance and social levels relative to the same category, allowing more metric variety within a certain group of pets. This means in the following diagram, that the Grey Parrot is not one of the most social pets but rather one of the most social *birds*.

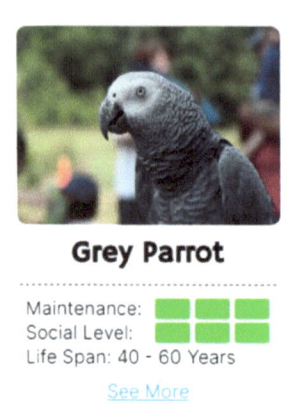

**Grey Parrot**

Maintenance: 🟩🟩🟩
Social Level: 🟩🟩🟩
Life Span: 40 - 60 Years

See More

**Budgerigar**

Maintenance: 🟥
Social Level: 🟩🟩🟩
Life Span: 5 - 8 Years

See More

Another problem I ran into was the high variation of what sources said a pet might cost monthly. For instance, one source estimated the monthly cost of a Labrador Retriever to be anywhere between $88 and $833. This proved to be problematic, as my code required each pet have a single value for price per month, rather than a range of values.

What is the Cost of Owning a Labrador Retriever per Month? **Generally, it is more expensive to own a dog** during their first year as the dog needs more veterinarian care. Owning a family Labrador retriever will cost between $1,060 to $10,000 annually or between **$88 to $833 a month**. The most expensive part of owning a Labrador retriever is their veterinary care.

The solution for this was to simply check more sources and see what the price averaged out to, though this was extremely time consuming.

An additional problem I encountered was conflicting sources. This was particularly prevalent when researching whether dogs could be vegan. One source would confidently claim they could, but a few links down, one insists they can't.

Like the previous problem I encountered, I simply went with whatever more sources claimed. My decision to consider dogs as vegan diet compatible came primarily from articles by `petkeen.com` and `petmd.com`.

## 4.4 Conclusion

The final product was very close to what I wanted, and nearly identical to the design I prototyped on Figma. One thing that I'm particularly proud of is the UI design. The idea for this UI was created entirely by me, with almost no inspiration taken from anywhere else.

There is a lot that may go unnoticed at first glance, like the drop shadow that was placed on the boxes of the pet cards that are colored green, yellow, and red. If you take a close look at the card of a pet with a maintenance or social level of 2 or less, you will notice the drop shadow is only present on the colored boxes, not the grey ones. Additionally, most colors are custom and chosen by me, like the color of the header and footer, or the links present on the page.

That being said, I can foresee potential improvements being made including more pets, more parameters for the user to enter, custom pages for each animal, and hosting on a custom domain. For now, you can access the project at `https://sohezee.github.io/`, along with the code at `https://github.com/Sohezee/PetPicker/`.

## Biography

Soham Vij is a high school student interested in the field of computer science. His fascination with computer science started from a young age, starting with Scratch in elementary school. Since then, he has self-studied Java, gotten the Oracle Java SE 8 certification (from the 1Z0-808 exam), taken web development and data analytics courses through local colleges, and am now learning more about HTML, CSS, and JavaScript via a Codecademy course. He plans to continue learning about computer science and pursue a career in it. Pet Picker was his first project using HTML, CSS and JavaScript. Soham hopes to not only expand this project but also make many more like this, all of which will be visible on his GitHub, `https://github.com/Sohezee`. If you would like to reach out to him for collaborations, questions, or opportunities, you can email him at `svij024@gmail.com`.

# About the Editors

**Sarasa Ouchi** is a 12th grader who loves baking. She co-founded AnimalHack and co-chaired its inaugural edition in 2023. A complete beginner in programming, she immersed herself in the world of computer science since experiencing Internet of Things with Python and Raspberry Pi. From then on, she regularly teaches Python coding and Internet of Things to K-12 students while continuing to hone her skills by organizing and participating in hackathons and taking computer science courses at school and online. She is fascinated by the wide range of applications that computer science can realize. Sarasa has won a Global Finalist Honorable Mention at the 2023 NASA Space Apps Challenge. She has also won an Ambassador Award in the National Community Service Awards program, which is sponsored by the United Nations Association of the USA. Sarasa holds an entry-level programming certification awarded by the Python Institute.

**Yuma Karube** is a 10th-grader who likes to read books and play video games. He co-founded AnimalHack and co-chaired its inaugural edition in 2023. By immersing himself in the world of the Internet of Things and teaching K-12 students Python programming and electrical engineering, he regularly develops his skills in Python and leadership. He even got his service recognized by the President of the United States and received a Gold Medal on the President's Volunteer Service Award in 2023. He is passionate about learning more about computer science because of how interesting and how it can be applied to a wide range of problems. Yuma has been actively going to one of the best STEM high schools in the nation and is a Certified Entry-Level Python Programmer.

**Banari Ouchi** is an 11th grader who enjoys drawing and playing video games. He co-founded AnimalHack and designed the cover of this book. Inspired by his sister, he started active participation in hackathons while taking programming courses at school and online. He has won a few awards for his hackathon projects on Internet of Things, including a Global Finalist Honorable Mention at the 2023 NASA Space Apps Challenge. Banri is also keen to serve youth communities with his technical knowledge and experience. He regularly teaches Python coding, cloud data storage and electronics to regional, nation-wide and international K-12 students. Banri is a Certified Entry-Level Python Programmer.

www.ingramcontent.com/pod-product-compliance
Lightning Source LLC
Chambersburg PA
CBHW050815290526
45792CB00001B/124